D1711984

About the Book

Everyday all around you, gravity is at work. Your hat stays on your head. Your books stay on your desk. And you stay on the ground.

Through observation and simple discussion, Melvin Berger explores gravity and its effect on our world and outer space. Boys and girls will be fascinated by his lucid explanation of weightlessness and rocket travel, and Arthur Schaffert's meaningful illustrations will extend their understanding of gravity.

The *Science Is What and Why* books present the fundamentals of science to young boys and girls. Interesting topics which are introduced in the elementary classroom are expanded and explored. These books, which have been checked for scientific accuracy by an authority, serve as excellent supplementary material.

GRAVITY

BY MELVIN BERGER
Illustrated by Arthur Schaffert

Coward-McCann, Inc.   New York

General Editor: Margaret Farrington Bartlett
Consultant: Theodore D. Johnson
Montclair Public Schools

GRAVITY

Jump as high as you can.
Why don't you fly off into space?

Lift a big stone.
Why does it feel heavy?

6

Put on your hat.
Why does it rest on your head?

Pick up a pencil and then let it go.
Why does the pencil fall?

Gravity!

Gravity is a force
that pulls down on everything.
It pulls all things down to earth.

7

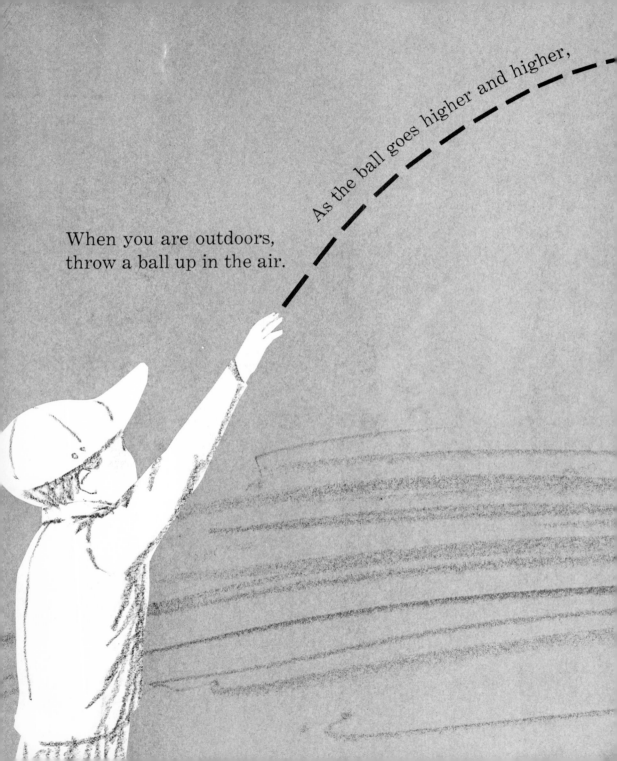

As the ball goes higher and higher,

When you are outdoors,
throw a ball up in the air.

it moves slower and slower.

Then it starts to fall.
The ball falls faster and faster
as it comes down.
The pull of gravity slows the ball on the way up,
and speeds it on the way down.

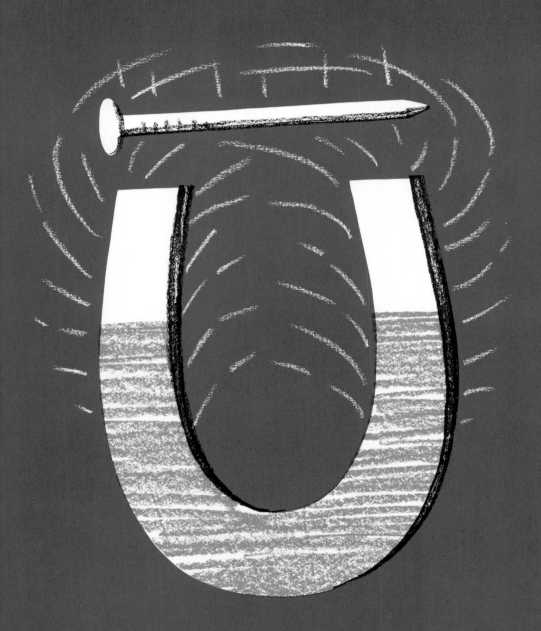

10

No one can see the pull of gravity.
It is something like the pull of a magnet
on a piece of iron.
The iron is pulled to the magnet.
You cannot see what pulls the iron to the magnet.
In the same way,
you cannot see the pull of gravity
on things to the earth.

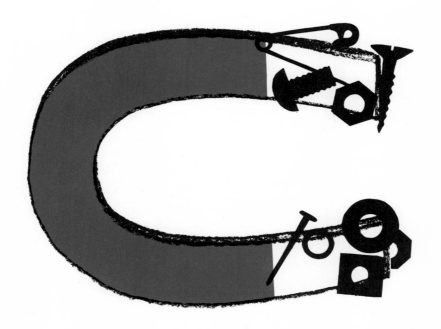

The earth is almost the shape of an orange.
People are standing up all over the earth.

12

No one falls off
  because gravity pulls everything
toward the center of the earth.
It pulls everybody and everything.
It pulls all the time.

Tie a key to a piece of string.
Hold one end of the string,
and let the key hang down.
The key points to the center of the earth.

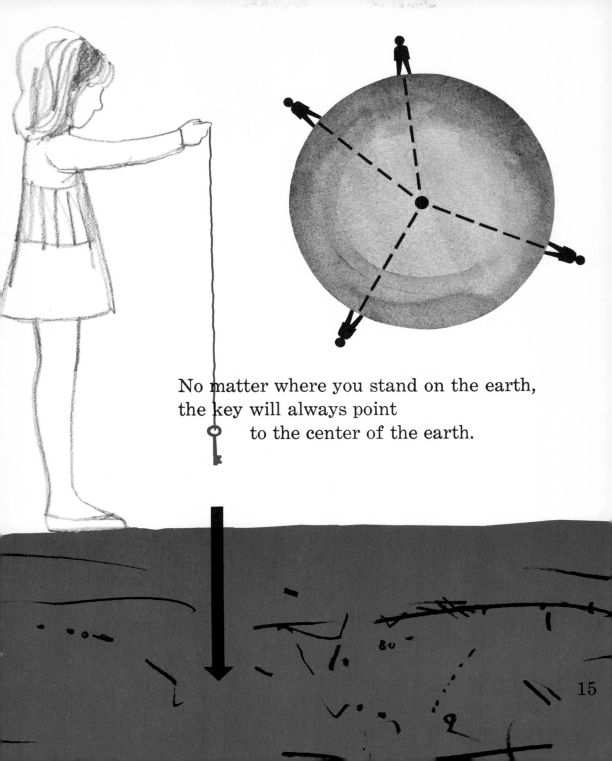

No matter where you stand on the earth,
the key will always point
to the center of the earth.

15

Put a book on a table.
Gravity holds it on the table.
Gravity pulls the book down.
Put the book on a scale.
Again gravity pulls the book down.
But this time you can measure
            the pull of gravity.

16

How many pounds does the book weigh?
The weight of the book is the force of gravity
pulling on the book.

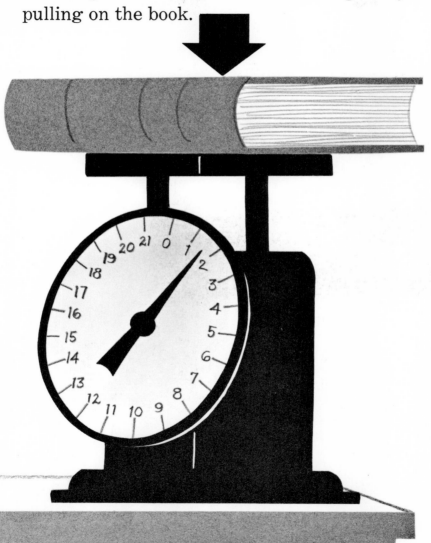

When you weigh anything,
you are measuring the pull of gravity.
Suppose you weigh 70 pounds.
That means that gravity
is pulling on you
with a force of 70 pounds.

70 lbs.

For a long time people thought about flying
far away from earth.
But they knew that gravity held them close to earth.
They had no way to overcome the force of gravity's pull.
"Whatever goes up must come down," they said.

Finally, not very long ago,
scientists found a way
to escape earth's gravity.

They invented a rocket
with a powerful engine.

The force of the engine
pushing the rocket up
was greater than the force
of gravity pulling it down.

The rocket was able to fly
out into space.

Attach a small ball to the end of a long rubber band.
Spin the ball around your head.
Spin it faster and faster.
If the ball reaches a certain speed,
the rubber band will tear.
The ball will fly away.

The rubber band is like gravity pulling on the ball.
The ball is like the rocket.
At slow speeds the rocket cannot break
free of gravity.
But if it is moving fast enough,
it breaks free,
and flies off into space.

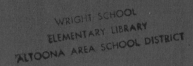
23

Astronauts have been on some of these rockets.
The rocket's engine pushes the rocket up into space.
At the same time, gravity pulls it down.

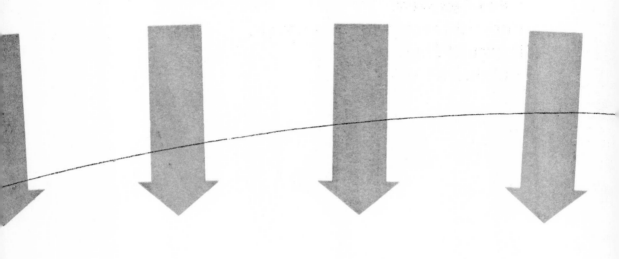

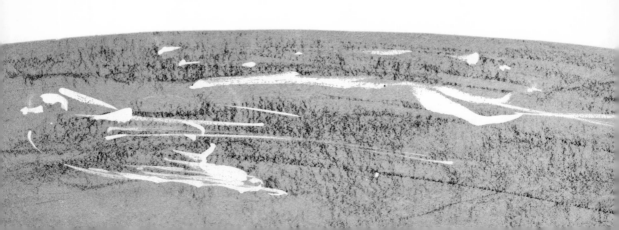

When the rocket reaches a speed
of about 17,000 miles per hour,
the forward push of the rocket
is the same as the downward pull of gravity.
It goes into an orbit around the earth.

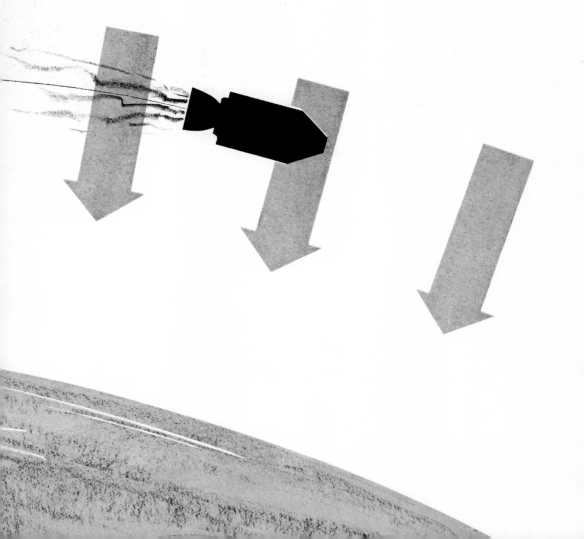

The rocket and the astronauts
do not feel the pull of gravity.
And without the pull of gravity they have no weight.
They are weightless.

If the astronauts are not strapped into their seats,
they float about the cabin.
If they let go of a pencil,
it hangs in space.
They have to squeeze food out of tubes into their mouths,
because the food would float off a plate.

To return to earth,
the astronauts fire rockets
that push them toward earth.

The pull of earth's gravity
then brings them down to earth.

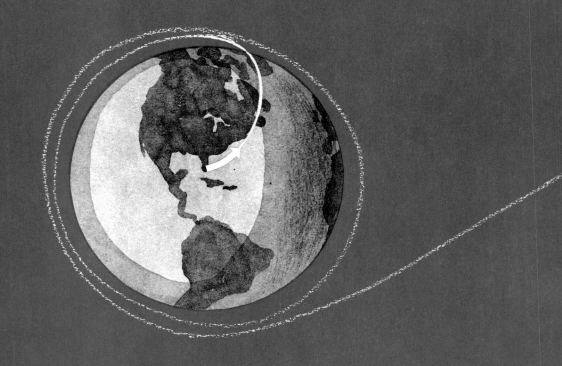

Now rockets can take astronauts to the moon.
Once there,
they are pulled to the moon by the moon's gravity.
The moon pulls all things down to its center,
just as the earth does.

Suppose that one day you travel in a rocket to the moon.
The rocket will need enough force
to travel at 25,000 miles per hour.
At this speed it can completely escape earth's gravity.

The weightless rocket will move toward the moon.
As it nears the moon,
the moon's gravity will take over.
The rocket will be pulled down to the moon.

33

The pull of the moon's gravity is much less
than the pull of earth's gravity.
The less the pull,
the less the weight.
If you weigh 70 pounds on earth,

70 lbs.

12 lbs.

you will weigh less
than 12 pounds on the moon.

You will be able to pick up huge rocks.

You will feel light and bouncy.
You will be able to jump higher
than you did on earth.
If you fall, you won't hurt yourself.

To return to earth,
rockets must be fired to get the spaceship
away from the moon's gravity.
The spaceship will move through space.

As it nears earth,
there will be a danger of crashing
because of the strong pull of earth's gravity.
Rockets will have to be fired to push against gravity.
This will slow down the spaceship,
and you will land safely.

After being weightless in space,
it will feel good to be home again.

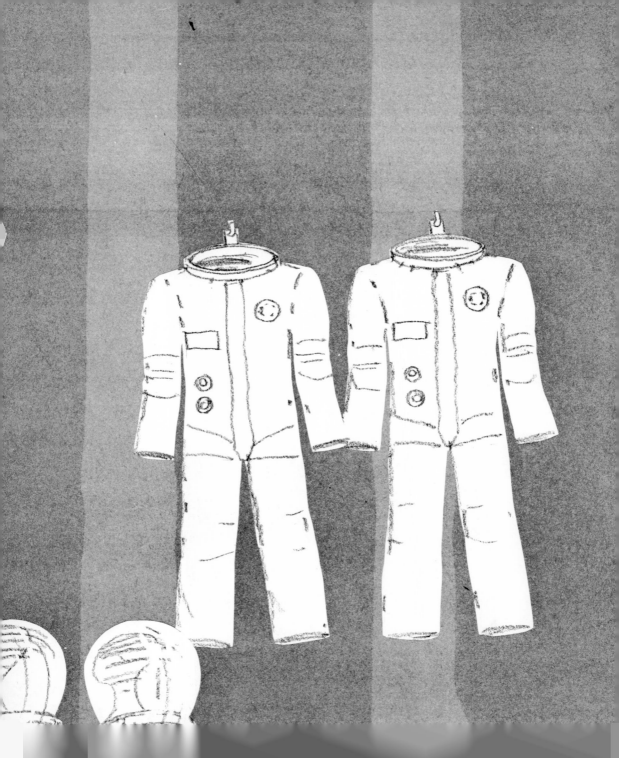

How wonderful it is to feel
the familiar pull of earth's gravity.
How wonderful it is to know
that gravity keeps everything in order on earth—
    —to know that you will not fall out into space
      when you jump,
    —to know that the ball you toss up
      will come down again,
    —and to know that your dinner will stay on the plate
      until you eat it.

We all need gravity.
We all depend on gravity.
Without gravity
this would be a topsy-turvy world!

46

About the Author

Melvin Berger presently lives in Great Neck, New York, with his family. He teaches science in the Plainview public schools.

A graduate of the University of Rochester, he did graduate work at Teacher's College, Columbia University, and at the University of London in England.

Mr. Berger is the author of ATOMS in the *Science Is What and Why* series plus three science books for boys and girls and a number of scientific articles for magazine publication.

About the Artist

Arthur Schaffert lives with his wife in Westport, Connecticut. Originally from Youngstown, Ohio, he was graduated from Carnegie Tech in Pittsburgh and Teacher's College, Columbia University.

He has taught design and handicrafts as well as contributed drawings to the Sunday magazine of the New York *Times* and many magazine publications. Mr. Schaffert illustrated ATOMS in this series.

Science Is What and Why

Each book in the *Science Is What and Why* series introduces fundamentals of science using a simple, attractive approach specifically designed for young boys and girls. Straightforward, lively language and distinguished illustrations which are a practical extension of the text present scientific facts as fascinating and exciting as the realm of the imagination.

RAIN AND THE VALLEY
by EDITH THACHER HURD
Illustrated by Clement Hurd

SEASHELL TOWNS
by PETER SAUER
Illustrated by Mark Binn

MAGNETS
by RAYMOND SACKS
Illustrated by Stefan Martin

FRICTION
by HOWARD LISS
Illustrated by Joseph Low

TELEPHONES
by BERNICE KOHN
Illustrated by Joseph Low

LEVERS
by BERNICE KOHN
Illustrated by Sean Morrison

ECHOES
by BERNICE KOHN
Illustrated by Albert Pucci

ELECTRICITY
by BEN KERNER
Illustrated by Mehlli Gobhai

WHEELS
by LISA MILLER
Illustrated by Tomie de Paola

HEAT
by HOWARD LISS
Illustrated by Abner Graboff

SOUND
by LISA MILLER
Illustrated by Tomie de Paola

LIGHT
by BERNICE KOHN
Illustrated by Janina Domanska

ATOMS
by MELVIN BERGER
Illustrated by Arthur Schaffert

MOTION
by SEYMOUR SIMON
Illustrated by Mehlli Gobhai

GRAVITY
by MELVIN BERGER
Illustrated by Arthur Schaffert

SEASONS
by PETER SAUER
Illustrated by John Kaufmann